A GUIDE TO

THE TEMPEST

The Shakespeare Handbooks

Guides available now:

- Antony & Cleopatra
- As You Like It
- Hamlet
- Henry IV, Part 1
- King Lear
- Macbeth
- A Midsummer Night's Dream
- Romeo & Juliet
- The Tempest
- Twelfth Night

Further titles in preparation.

The Shakespeare Handbooks

A Guide to
The Tempest

Alistair McCallum

Upstart Crow Publications

First published in 2016 by
Upstart Crow Publications

Copyright © Alistair McCallum 2016

ISBN 978 1 899747 08 5

www.shakespeare-handbooks.com

Setting the scene

Shakespeare wrote *The Tempest* during the period 1610–11. He was in his late forties, and had been one of England's foremost dramatists for the past twenty years. He was a member and shareholder of the King's Men, the country's most prestigious theatre company. The company's chief patron was King James I, a great lover of the theatre, and they gave frequent performances at court.

The Tempest was Shakespeare's last play written single-handedly; after this time, he worked in collaboration with younger playwrights, and he seems to have retired from the theatre altogether a few years later.

It is difficult to classify *The Tempest*. The four plays written towards the end of Shakespeare's career – *Pericles*, *The Winter's Tale*, *Cymbeline* and *The Tempest* – are variously referred to as the Late Comedies, the Tragicomedies, or the Romances. These plays share a number of themes: long, arduous journeys; potentially tragic situations that are resolved happily; elements of magic and the supernatural; the reuniting of long-separated family members; and eventual homecoming, reconciliation, and redemption. *The Tempest* is generally regarded as the greatest of these four late plays.

This enigmatic, strangely powerful play has served as the inspiration for countless other works of art, including operas, orchestral works, songs, novels, poetry and painting. Films based on *The Tempest* range from silent versions of the early 20th century to *Forbidden Planet* and *Prospero's Books* later in the century.

Exactly why Shakespeare turned away from tragedy and towards more mystical themes at this stage of his life is not known. The results, however, were every bit as compelling as anything that had come before:

"After progressively more successful attempts – in Pericles, Cymbeline *and* The Winter's Tale *– at mingling elements of tragedy and comedy within a framework of magic and exoticism taken from literary romances, the playwright created in* The Tempest *a stunning theatrical entertainment that is also a moral allegory of great beauty and emotional power."*

Charles Boyce, *Shakespeare A to Z*

Danger at sea

A fleet of ships, heading home across the Mediterranean Sea to Naples, has been caught in a sudden storm. On board one of the vessels is Alonso, King of Naples.

The passengers on Alonso's ship include his brother Sebastian, his son Ferdinand, and various members of the King's court. Also travelling with the royal party is Antonio, Duke of Milan.

The storm is getting more and more violent with every passing minute.

Curtain up

Disaster is imminent

On board the King's ship, amidst the howling winds and mountainous waves, the crew are desperately trying to keep control and prevent the ship from crashing on the shore of a nearby island.

The King himself is on deck, along with his companions, including Duke Antonio. The King and the Duke both insist on talking to the ship's master: but the boatswain, busy attending to the master's orders, and shouting commands in turn to the mariners, has no time for his passengers' demands. He tells them, bluntly, to go down to their cabins.

Gonzalo, the King's adviser, tries to calm the boatswain's temper, but his words are brushed aside:

Antonio: Where is the master, boatswain?

Boatswain: Do you not hear him? You mar our labour. Keep your cabins! You do assist the storm.

Gonzalo: Nay, good,[1] be patient.

Boatswain: When the sea is! Hence. What cares these roarers[2] for the name of king? To cabin! Silence! Trouble us not.

Gonzalo: Good, yet remember whom thou hast aboard.

Boatswain: None that I more love than myself. You are a councillor; if you can command these elements to silence and work[3] the peace of the present, we will not hand a rope more. Use your authority! If you cannot, give thanks you have lived so long and make yourself ready in your cabin for the mischance of the hour, if it so hap ... Out of our way, I say!

[1] *good man*
[2] *roaring, violent waves*
[3] *achieve, bring about*

As the boatswain hurries away, Gonzalo remarks sardonically that the man's lack of respect may be a good omen: his destiny is clearly to be hanged, not drowned.

The boatswain returns, still bellowing orders to the crew. He is exasperated to find some of the passengers still on deck. The King's brother Sebastian and the Duke, infuriated by the man's lack of respect, hurl insults at him:

Boatswain: Yet again? What do you here? Shall we give o'er and drown? Have you a mind to sink?
Sebastian: A pox o'your throat, you bawling, blasphemous, incharitable dog.
Boatswain: Work you, then.
Antonio: Hang, cur! Hang, you whoreson, insolent noise-maker! We are less afraid to be drowned than thou art.

At this point some mariners rush in: there is no hope of saving the ship, they tell the boatswain. The only thing left to do is to pray. From within the ship, screams and cries for help are heard. Still cursing at the boatswain, Sebastian and Antonio go down to join the King and his son, who are praying in their cabin.

Gonzalo reflects that this is not the death he would have chosen:

Gonzalo: Now would I give a thousand furlongs of sea for an acre of barren ground … The wills above be done, but I would fain[1] die a dry death.

[1] *willingly*

A revelation

A young woman, Miranda, has been watching the terrible storm and shipwreck from the safety of the island. She is dismayed at the ferocity of the tempest and the suffering of the victims.

Also watching the scene is Miranda's father Prospero, wearing the robes of a magician. Aware of her father's potent magical powers, Miranda is anxious that, if he created the storm for some reason, he should bring it to an end at once:

Miranda: If by your art,[1] my dearest father, you have
Put the wild waters in this roar, allay them.
                   … O, I have suffered
With those that I saw suffer – a brave vessel
(Who had no doubt some noble creature in her)
Dashed all to pieces. O, the cry did knock
Against my very heart! Poor souls, they perished.

[1] *magic*

Prospero reassures his tearful daughter that no one has come to any harm. In fact, the storm they have witnessed is part of a plan created with her in mind.

"There are parallels between Prospero's art of magic and the art of the theater … We think we are in the middle of a 'real' storm, but the next scene reveals that this was a theatrical illusion, magicked up by Prospero from the island to bring his enemies into his power. The seafarers were never in danger: the events looked believable but were created out of a few props and a believable script. As in a play, events happen, controlled by an unseen dramatist, to further a yet unknown plot. Throughout the play Prospero controls the other characters like a playwright …"

Laurie Maguire and Emma Smith, *30 Great Myths about Shakespeare*, 2013

Prospero admits to his daughter that he has kept her in ignorance of her background. Who she is, who Prospero is, how and why they came to settle on this remote island; none of this has been explained to Miranda. The time has now come, decides Prospero, for her to learn the truth. Removing his magician's robe, he asks her to sit down, and questions her about her early memories:

Prospero: Canst thou remember
A time before we came unto this cell?[1]
I do not think thou canst, for then thou wast not
Out[2] three years old.

[1] *simple dwelling-place*
[2] *not yet*

To Prospero's surprise, Miranda claims she can remember something of her life before coming to the island. She has a hazy recollection, she says, of being cared for by a group of four or five women. Prospero is curious to know what else she remembers:

Prospero: But how is it
That this lives in thy mind? What seest thou else
In the dark backward and abysm of time?

But Miranda can remember nothing more of her earliest years, or of their journey to the island. Prospero now breaks some momentous news to her:

Prospero: Twelve year since,[1] Miranda, twelve year since,
Thy father was the Duke of Milan, and
A prince of power.

[1] *ago*

Miranda is confused; surely Prospero, sitting in front of her, is her father? It is the truth, says Prospero: he was the Duke, and Miranda, his only child, his rightful heir. It was treachery that brought about their exile from Milan, but fortune treated them kindly in delivering them to their new home:

Miranda: O, the heavens!
What foul play had we that we came from thence?
Or blessed was't we did?

Prospero: Both, both, my girl.
By foul play, as thou sayst, were we heaved thence,
But blessedly holp hither.[1]

[1] *helped on our way here*

The overthrow of the rightful Duke

Instructing Miranda to listen carefully, Prospero now describes the events that brought him and his infant daughter to the island that was to become their home.

He recalls that Milan was the greatest of the Italian city-states and that he, as Duke, was renowned for his learning. In fact, his pursuit of knowledge was so consuming that he eventually left the business of government to his beloved brother Antonio:

Prospero: Through all the signories[1] it was the first,
And Prospero the prime Duke, being so reputed
In dignity, and for the liberal arts
Without a parallel; those being all my study,
The government I cast upon my brother
And to my state grew stranger, being transported
And rapt in secret studies.

[1] *republics, city-states*

... to my state grew stranger, being transported
And rapt in secret studies.

Prospero's description of his downfall could be seen as a tribute to King James I, patron of the theatre company of which Shakespeare had been a member for many years.

In a book written originally for his son, the King gives advice for becoming a just, benevolent and efficient monarch. At one point he provides a warning which would have been valuable to Shakespeare's Duke of Milan:

"... it is necessarie yee delight in reading, and seeking the knowledge of all lawfull things; but with these two restrictions: first, that ye choose idle houres for it, not interrupting therewith the discharge of your office: and next, that yee studie not for knowledge nakedly, but that your principall ende be, to make you able thereby to use your office."

King James I, *Basilikon Doron*, 1603

Prospero's brother proved to be an adept, cunning politician, and soon exploited his power to ensure that Prospero's followers became loyal – through fear or greed – to Antonio. Eventually Prospero was rendered virtually powerless:

Prospero: Being once perfected how to grant suits,[1]
How to deny them, who t'advance and who
To trash for overtopping,[2] new created
The creatures that were mine[3] ...
                    ... now he was
The ivy which had hid my princely trunk
And sucked my verdure[4] out on't.

[1] *requests for favours*
[2] *to suppress for being over-ambitious*
[3] *gained the loyalty of those who owed their success to me*
[4] *vitality, vigour*

Despite Antonio's ever-increasing influence, Prospero's trust in his brother was undiminished, and he remained devoted to his life of scholarship. Finally, however, Antonio's desire for money and power led him to one goal: he wanted nothing less than the Dukedom of Milan for himself.

To achieve his ambition, Antonio colluded with Milan's old enemy, the King of Naples. They came to a pact: if Antonio agreed to make Milan the subject state of Naples, and to make an annual payment, then the King would raise an army, invade the city of Milan, and install Antonio as Duke in his brother's place.

Miranda is horrified that Prospero's brother could be so wicked and deceitful. It is almost as if he were not her father's true brother, something which she refuses to believe:

Prospero: … then tell me
                    If this might be a brother.
Miranda: I should sin
                    To think but[1] nobly of my grandmother;
                    Good wombs have borne bad sons.

    [1] *anything other than*

The troops sent from Naples arrived late one night, as planned, and Antonio opened the gates of Milan to them. Prospero and Miranda were hurriedly removed from the city by Antonio's officials.

Aware of Prospero's popularity among the city's inhabitants, Antonio decided against putting him and his daughter to death. Instead, a ship took them several miles out into the Mediterranean; they were then put on board a decrepit old boat and cast out to sea.

Miranda, remembering nothing of the events, tries to imagine her father's suffering:

Prospero: ... they prepared
A rotten carcass of a butt,[1] not rigged,
Nor tackle, sail, nor mast – the very rats
Instinctively have quit it. There they hoist us
To cry to th' sea that roared to us ...
Miranda: Alack, what trouble
Was I then to you?
Prospero: O, a cherubin
Thou wast that did preserve me. Thou didst smile,
Infused with a fortitude from heaven ...

[1] *tub, cask*

The man given the task of taking Prospero and his daughter out to sea was one of the King's advisers, a man named Gonzalo. Prospero recalls that, although he did his duty, he showed great kindness, making sure that the castaway pair had a supply of food, fresh water and clothes. Most importantly, he remembered Prospero's love of learning:

Prospero: ... of his gentleness,
Knowing I loved my books, he furnished me
From mine own library with volumes that
I prize above my dukedom.

So it was, concludes Prospero, that the two of them came to be on this remote island. Miranda has one more question for her father: why did he create the dreadful storm that she has just witnessed? Prospero hints that fate has been kind to him:

Prospero: ... By accident most strange, bountiful fortune
(Now my dear lady) hath mine enemies
Brought to this shore ...

The two men who conspired against him, his brother and the King of Naples, are now on the island, and under his power. An opportunity to right the wrongs of the past has arisen; Prospero must seize it.

A successful mission

The story has come to an end and, at her father's command, Miranda falls into a deep sleep.

Prospero now calls for his servant Ariel, an airy spirit being who can take on an infinite variety of shapes and disguises:

Prospero: I am ready now.
                  Approach, my Ariel. Come.
Ariel: All hail, great master; grave sir, hail! I come
                  To answer thy best pleasure, be't to fly,
                  To swim, to dive into the fire, to ride
                  On the curled clouds.

Ariel confirms that, as commanded, he created a terrifying storm around King Alonso's ship. He reassures his master that no one has been harmed; the passengers, who all jumped into the sea in their panic, have been brought safely to various parts of the island, while the crew are sleeping soundly below decks. The ship itself is anchored securely in one of the island's coves:

Ariel: Safely in harbour
          Is the King's ship, in the deep nook where once
          Thou called'st me up at midnight to fetch dew
          From the still-vexed[1] Bermudas; there she's hid,
          The mariners all under hatches stowed ...

    [1]   *constantly wild and stormy*

The other ships in the fleet, scattered by the storm, have regrouped. Having witnessed the disaster that struck King Alonso's ship, which no one could be expected to survive, they have continued on their journey, taking the sad news of the King's death to Naples.

... the still-vexed Bermudas ...

In 1609, the *Sea Venture* was sent by the Virginia Company of London to carry supplies across the Atlantic to the newly-established colony of Jamestown. The ship was caught in a terrible storm, and attempted to take refuge near an island, as one of the passengers, William Strachey, later recounted:

"For foure and twenty houres the storme in a restlesse tumult, had blown so exceedingly, as we could not apprehend in our imaginations any possibility of greater violence, yet wee did still finde it ... we were inforced to runne her ashoare, as neere the land as we could ... We found it to be the dangerous and dreaded Iland, or rather Ilands of the Bermuda *... because they be so terrible to all that ever touched on them, and such tempests, thunders, and other fearfull objects are seene and heard about them, that they be called commonly,* The Devil's Ilands*, and are feared and avoyded of all sea travellers alive, above any other place in the world."*

Eventually the captain was forced to run the ship aground on the island's rocky coast. Astonishingly, all 150 people on board – and even the ship's dog – were landed safely. They spent several months on the island while new ships were constructed, and eventually completed their journey to Virginia. Contrary to its notorious reputation, Bermuda was found to be pleasant, temperate and fertile.

Back in London, news of the crew's survival created great excitement. An unpublished draft of Strachey's report reached London in 1610, and was almost certainly seen by Shakespeare, some of whose acquaintances were involved in the Virginia Company. The story clearly caught his imagination, and provided material for the opening scenes of *The Tempest*; indeed, it may have been the inspiration for the entire play.

Ariel is reminded of his past

Prospero tells Ariel that, with the ship's passengers safely on shore, there is a lot to do in the next few hours. Ariel protests, and his master in turn becomes angry:

> *Ariel:* Is there more toil? Since thou dost give me pains,
> Let me remember [1] thee what thou hast promised,
> Which is not yet performed me.
> *Prospero:* How now? Moody?
> What is't thou canst demand?
> *Ariel:* My liberty.
>
> [1] *remind*

One day, Prospero has promised, Ariel will be set free, and will no longer have a master to obey. That time has not yet come, he insists. Ariel reminds him that, in return for his honest, willing service, Prospero had agreed to shorten his period of servitude. In response, Prospero angrily reminds Ariel of the events of the past, and the dreadful suffering from which the spirit was rescued.

An evil witch named Sycorax was banished from Algiers for her malicious activities; she was pregnant, and the authorities did not put her to death, abandoning her instead on this remote, uninhabited island. She made Ariel her servant, but the spirit refused to take part in her wicked schemes. He was punished severely for his disobedience:

> *Prospero:* ... thou wast a spirit too delicate
> To act her earthy and abhorred commands,
> Refusing her grand hests [1] – she did confine thee,
> By help of her more potent ministers
> And in her most unmitigable rage,
> Into a cloven pine, [2] within which rift
> Imprisoned thou didst painfully remain
> A dozen years ...
>
> [1] *imperious orders*
> [2] *a pine tree that she had split open*

Sycorax died, leaving her brutish, half-human son Caliban as the island's only inhabitant. It was not until the arrival of Prospero, with his magical powers, that Ariel was finally released from his painful imprisonment:

> *Prospero:*   Thou best knowst
> What torment I did find thee in: thy groans
> Did make wolves howl and penetrate the breasts
> Of ever-angry bears. It was a torment
> To lay upon the damned, which Sycorax
> Could not again undo. It was mine art,
> When I arrived and heard thee, that made gape
> The pine and let thee out.

Ariel apologises for his impudence. Then, to his delight, Prospero reveals that he will be freed in a matter of days. He eagerly accepts his next task; for this, Prospero explains, he will need to transform himself into a sea-nymph, invisible to everyone except his master.

As Ariel leaves to prepare for his task, Miranda wakes from her deep sleep. Prospero tells her that he needs to talk to the ill-tempered Caliban:

> *Prospero:* We'll visit Caliban, my slave, who never
> Yields us kind answer.
> *Miranda:*   'Tis a villain, sir,
> I do not love to look on.
> *Prospero:*   But as 'tis,
> We cannot miss [1] him; he does make our fire,
> Fetch in our wood, and serves in offices
> That profit us.
>
> [1] *do without*

Prospero calls for his slave. Caliban's hostile voice is heard, but before he arrives Ariel returns, visible only to his master. Prospero whispers his instructions to the spirit, and Ariel sets off on his mission.

An unwilling helper

Prospero calls again for Caliban. When he finally arrives, the mutual loathing between them is immediately apparent:

Prospero: Thou poisonous slave, got[1] by the devil himself
Upon thy wicked dam;[2] come forth!

Caliban: As wicked dew as ere my mother brushed
With raven's feather from unwholesome fen[3]
Drop on you both.

[1] conceived
[2] mother
[3] swamp

Prospero warns Caliban that he will be punished for his hostility and his laziness with aches, cramps and stings all night.

Caliban replies that the island is rightfully his, inherited from his mother; he should not be obliged to serve Prospero. He remembers how different things were when Prospero first arrived:

Caliban: … This island's mine, by Sycorax my mother,
Which thou tak'st from me. When thou cam'st first
Thou strok'st me and made much of me; wouldst give me
Water with berries in't, and teach me how
To name the bigger light and how the less
That burn by day and night. And then I loved thee
And showed thee all the qualities o'th' isle:
The fresh springs, brine pits, barren place and fertile.
Cursed be I that did so!

In the 1970s, a copy of the complete works of Shakespeare was smuggled into the prison on South Africa's Robben Island, which held many political prisoners including Nelson Mandela. The book, which became known as the 'Robben Island Bible', was passed around secretly from cell to cell, and many prisoners underlined passages in the text that they found particularly significant.

The anti-apartheid activist Billy Nair, imprisoned for twenty years and frequently beaten by his jailers, chose one of Caliban's speeches from *The Tempest:*

> *This island's mine, by Sycorax my mother,*
> *Which thou tak'st from me ...*

Now, by contrast, Caliban finds himself a virtual prisoner, living in a squalid cave and labouring for Prospero and his daughter.

Prospero furiously reminds Caliban that he brought about his own disgrace when he attempted to rape Miranda:

Prospero:	Thou most lying slave,
	Whom stripes [1] may move, not kindness; I have used thee,
	Filth as thou art, with humane care and lodged thee
	In mine own cell, till thou didst seek to violate
	The honour of my child.
Caliban:	O ho, O ho! Would't had been done;
	Thou didst prevent me, I had peopled else [2]
	This isle with Calibans.

[1] *lashes, whipping*
[2] *otherwise I would have populated*

Miranda too had taken pity on Caliban at first, and had taught him to speak:

Miranda: Abhorred slave,
Which any print of goodness wilt not take,[1]
Being capable of all ill; I pitied thee,
Took pains to make thee speak, taught thee each hour
One thing or other …

Caliban: You taught me language, and my profit on't
Is I know how to curse. The red plague[2] rid[3] you
For learning me your language.

[1] *who cannot be imprinted with virtue*
[2] *plague that produces red sores*
[3] *destroy*

Prospero orders Caliban to fetch some firewood. The creature's reluctance irritates Prospero, who again threatens him with pain and cramps. Caliban, all too aware of his master's magical powers, hurries away to carry out his chore.

An intriguing visitor

Ariel now returns, along with his fellow spirits. Invisible to all but Prospero, they are singing, and their music has attracted the attention of one of the victims of the shipwreck. It is Ferdinand, son of the King of Naples; enchanted, he has followed the sound towards Prospero's home.

Ferdinand: Sitting on a bank,
Weeping again[1] the King my father's wreck,
This music crept by me upon the waters,
Allaying both their fury and my passion
With its sweet air. Thence I have followed it …

[1] *over and over again*

Ariel now sings a strange, melancholy ballad:

Ariel: Full fathom five thy father lies,
               Of his bones are coral made;
               Those are pearls that were his eyes,
               Nothing of him that doth fade
               But doth suffer a sea-change
               Into something rich and strange.

Ferdinand cannot help thinking of his own father, the King, believing him to have drowned in the storm.

Time and again in Shakespeare we find vivid, striking words and phrases, coined by the author, that have since become part of the fabric of the English language. There are well over a thousand such original creations in Shakespeare's plays. In *The Tempest* alone, for example, we find:

> *sea-change*
> *strange bedfellows*
> *brave new world*
> *such stuff as dreams are made on*
> *melted into thin air*

In Shakespeare's time, English was in a state of flux; pronunciation, grammar and spelling were all much more flexible than they are in modern English. This gave the language an energy and inventiveness that still appeals to us:

"Elizabethan English, alone among the earlier stages of our language, still plays a part in modern intellectual life. Thanks to the English Bible, the prayer-book and Shakespeare, it has never become really obsolete ... Modern English is the fitting medium of an age which leaves little unexplained; while Elizabethan English stands for an age too hasty to analyse what it felt. The one has the virtues of maturity, a logic, uncompromising and clear: the other, a vigour and a felicity, the saving graces of youth."

A.W. Ward and A. R. Waller, *The Cambridge History of English and American Literature*, 1921

Unseen, Prospero and Miranda have been observing Ferdinand. Prospero is curious to know his daughter's reaction to the young man; she has never seen a human being other than himself and Caliban. Miranda is impressed, but unsure what to make of the new arrival:

Miranda:	What is't, a spirit?
	Lord, how it looks about. Believe me, sir,
	It carries a brave form. But 'tis a spirit.
Prospero:	No, wench, it eats and sleeps and hath such senses
	As we have ...
	... He hath lost his fellows
	And strays about to find 'em.
Miranda:	I might call him
	A thing divine, for nothing natural
	I ever saw so noble.

Prospero is pleased; everything is going according to plan.

Ferdinand is enchanted

Ferdinand suddenly catches sight of Miranda. His first thought is that this is the goddess for whom the ethereal music is intended. He questions her tentatively: is this island her home? How should he behave in this strange land? And is she indeed a goddess, or a mortal maid?

Miranda answers that she is human. Ferdinand is startled to hear her speak the same language as himself. He reflects that in his own country, amongst those who speak his language, he is the highest-ranking individual in the state. Prospero asks whether the King is not above him; Ferdinand explains, sadly, that his father the King perished in the storm, along with many other noblemen of Naples and Milan.

It soon becomes clear that, with Ariel's help, Ferdinand and Miranda have fallen instantly in love. Prospero congratulates his servant, and promises again that he will soon be set free. However, he does not want the lovers' path to be too smooth:

Prospero: [aside] They are both in either's powers: but this
                swift business
            I must uneasy make, lest too light[1] winning
            Make the prize light.[2]

[1] easy, effortless
[2] of little value

To Miranda's distress, her father starts to quarrel with the young man, accusing him of lying; he is an impostor whose aim is to take possession of the island. Prospero intends to put Ferdinand in chains and keep him captive.

"Prospero is the central figure of The Tempest; *and it has often been wildly asserted that he is a portrait of the author – an embodiment of that spirit of wise benevolence which is supposed to have thrown a halo over Shakespeare's later life. But, on closer inspection, the portrait seems to be as imaginary as the original. To an irreverent eye, the ex-Duke of Milan would perhaps appear as an unpleasantly crusty personage, in whom a twelve years' monopoly of the conversation had developed an inordinate propensity for talking ... it is sufficient to point out, that if Prospero is wise, he is also self-opinionated and sour, that his gravity is often another name for pedantic severity, and that there is no character in the play to whom, during some part of it, he is not studiously disagreeable."*

Lytton Strachey, *Shakespeare's Final
Period*, 1904

As the argument escalates, Ferdinand draws his sword; but, under Prospero's power, he finds himself suddenly unable to move.

Miranda pleads with her father, insisting that Ferdinand is a gentle, good man. Prospero scolds her for her naivety:

Prospero: Hush.
Thou think'st there is no more such shapes as he,
Having seen but him and Caliban. Foolish wench,
To[1] th' most of men, this is a Caliban,
And they to him are angels.
Miranda: My affections
Are then most humble. I have no ambition
To see a goodlier man.

> [1] *compared to*

Prospero orders Ferdinand to come with him to his place of imprisonment. Still under Prospero's spell, Ferdinand is unable to resist. He feels strangely calm; as long as he can see Miranda from time to time, he will be content.

Ferdinand: My spirits, as in a dream, are all bound up.
My father's loss, the weakness which I feel,
The wreck of all my friends, nor this man's threats
(To whom I am subdued) are but light to me,
Might I but[1] through my prison once a day
Behold this maid.

> [1] *as long as I might*

With a final word of thanks to the invisible Ariel, and a reprimand to Miranda for taking the young man's side, Prospero leaves. Ferdinand follows obediently.

Fifty years after Shakespeare's death, many of his plays remained popular. However, tastes had changed considerably in the intervening years, and it was generally agreed that his works were in need of revision and improvement. The playwright and poet John Dryden, a leading literary figure of Restoration England, summed up the general feeling of the time:

"... the tongue in general is so much refin'd since Shakespear's time, that many of his words, and more of his Phrases, are scarce intelligible. And of those which we understand, some are ungrammatical, others coarse; and his whole style is so pester'd with Figurative expressions, that it is as affected as it is obscure."

John Dryden, Preface to *Troilus and Cressida*, 1679

With the help of his friend Sir William D'Avenant, Dryden created *The Tempest, or The Enchanted Island*, an adaptation of Shakespeare's work. About two-thirds of the original text was cut. The new play included plenty of music, dancing and comedy, and several new characters were added; actresses could now appear on the public stage, something that would have been inconceivable in Shakespeare's day. Miranda was given a sister, as was Caliban; there was even an appearance by the airy female spirit Milcha, a sweetheart for Ariel.

This new play proved extremely popular. Samuel Pepys, an avid theatregoer, saw it at least ten times. His love of the theatre was almost obsessive; at one point, after six visits to the theatre in two weeks, he resolved to curb his habit, which was interfering with his work and getting him a reputation for idleness:

"... to the Duke of York's house, and there saw The Tempest *again, which is very pleasant, and full of so good variety that I cannot be more pleased almost in a comedy, only the seamen's part a little too tedious. Thence home, and there to my chamber, and do begin anew to bind myself to keep my old vows, and among the rest not to see a play till Christmas but once in every other week, and have laid aside 10 shillings, which is to be lost to the poor, if I do. This I hope in God will bind me, for I do find myself mightily wronged in my reputation, and indeed in my purse and business, by my late following of my pleasure for so long time as I have done."*

Samuel Pepys, diary entry for 13th November 1667

The King is grief-stricken

Ferdinand is not the only survivor of the shipwreck. On another part of the island is his father Alonso, King of Naples, accompanied by his friends and courtiers.

In the same group are the King's brother Sebastian and the Duke of Milan, Antonio, who ousted his brother Prospero many years ago. Unlike Alonso, they are untroubled by the situation, and the two of them comment mockingly on the solemn conversation of the others in the group. They are particularly amused by Gonzalo's unsuccessful attempts to console the King:

Gonzalo:	Beseech you, sir, be merry. You have cause
	(So have we all) of joy, for our escape
	Is much beyond our loss [1] ...
Alonso:	Prithee, peace. [2]
Sebastian:	[*to Antonio*] He receives comfort like cold porridge.
Antonio:	[*to Sebastian*] The visitor will not give him o'er so. [3]
Sebastian:	[*to Antonio*] Look, he's winding up the watch of his wit; by and by it will strike.

[1] *the fact that we have survived outweighs our losses*
[2] *leave me in peace, be silent*
[3] *his counsellor will not give up that easily*

Indifferent to Sebastian and Antonio's scornful comments, Gonzalo remarks that the island, though uninhabited, seems to be a pleasant, fertile place. Another thing that strikes him is the fact that their clothes seem unaffected by their recent drenching in sea-water. In passing, he mentions the reason for their journey across the Mediterranean:

Gonzalo:	Methinks our garments are now as fresh as
	when we put them on first in Africa, at the
	marriage of the King's fair daughter Claribel
	to the King of Tunis.

It was on the journey back from Tunis that the King's fleet encountered the terrible storm which brought them to this island. Alonso, hearing talk of the wedding, is overcome by emotion, certain that he will never see his son Ferdinand again:

Alonso: Would I had never
Married my daughter there, for coming thence [1]
My son is lost and (in my rate) she too,
Who is so far from Italy removed
I ne'er again shall see her. O thou mine heir
Of Naples and Milan, what strange fish
Hath made his meal on thee?

[1] *from there*

One of the King's courtiers tries to persuade him that Ferdinand may still be alive; he saw the young man fighting against the raging sea after abandoning the ship, and he may have managed to swim ashore. Alonso, however, has lost all hope of seeing him.

The King's brother Sebastian is unsympathetic. He tells Alonso, bluntly, that he has only himself to blame. Most of his family disapproved of the marriage of his daughter Claribel to the king of a distant African land; in fact, Claribel herself was unhappy about the match.

Alonso does not argue with his brother, but returns to his state of quiet despair. Gonzalo reproaches Sebastian respectfully:

Gonzalo: My lord Sebastian,
The truth you speak doth lack some gentleness,
And time to speak it in. [1] You rub the sore
When you should bring the plaster.

[1] *timeliness, appropriateness*

Gonzalo imagines a Golden Age

Gonzalo, still hoping to distract the King from his sorrow, starts musing aloud about ruling over the island:

Gonzalo: Had I plantation of this isle,[1] my lord ...
And were the king on't, what would I do?

[1] *If this island were my colony*

He starts to imagine a nation completely different from any in the known world:

Gonzalo: I'th' commonwealth I would by contraries[1]
Execute all things, for no kind of traffic[2]
Would I admit; no name of magistrate;
Letters[3] should not be known; riches, poverty
And use of service,[4] none ...

[1] *contrary to usual customs*
[2] *business, commerce*
[3] *reading, learning*
[4] *master and servant relationships*

He envisages a society without hierarchy, laws, or property. Warming to his theme, he goes even further: there should be no money, no agriculture, indeed no work of any kind, and people would live simply and effortlessly off the fruits of the earth.

Gonzalo: No occupation, all men idle, all;
And women, too, but innocent and pure;
No sovereignty –
Sebastian: Yet he would be king on't.
Antonio: The latter end of his commonwealth forgets
the beginning.

Gonzalo: All things in common nature should produce
Without sweat or endeavour; treason, felony,
Sword, pike, knife, gun, or need of any engine [1]
Would I not have; but nature should bring forth
Of its own kind [2] all foison, [3] all abundance,
To feed my innocent people.

[1] *military machinery*
[2] *by itself, without human interference*
[3] *profusion, harvest*

Sebastian and Antonio ridicule the old councillor and his ideas: while the King, still wrapped up in his sadness, is barely listening.

Had I plantation of this isle ...

Gonzalo's musings remind us that England in Shakespeare's time was at the dawn of an age of vigorous overseas exploration and colonization. England's last possessions in Europe had been lost long before, and attention was turning further afield, with the creation of the East India Company and the Virginia Company. The often painful incursion of the Old World of Europe into the New World of the Americas and the Caribbean was a subject of intense interest and debate:

"The time of The Tempest, *roughly 1611, was a time when Britain, having lost its toehold on the Continent fifty years back, was beginning, with the founding of the East India Company and the first tentative settlements in America, to think in terms of an overseas empire."*

Northrop Frye, *On Shakespeare*, 1986

> *"The play is fairly saturated with references to sleep and waking – and to various states of consciousness and unconsciousness between the two, drowsiness, daydreaming, dreaming, trance, hallucination ... Likewise,* The Tempest *is filled from end to end with noises and music – from the thunder and roaring of the storm itself, the howling of beasts, through the sounds and sweet airs of the Enchanted Isle ... Shakespeare seems interested not only in these two things, sleep and music, but in the relation between them – the relation between music and the unconscious mind."*
>
> Harold C. Goddard, *The Meaning of Shakespeare*, 1951

The King's life in danger

Ariel now approaches, unseen, playing solemn music. Gonzalo and the other lords fall asleep, and the King too starts to feel drowsy. Alonso hopes that sleep might allow him to escape from the troubled thoughts running continually through his mind. His brother and the Duke encourage him to give way to his drowsiness:

Alonso: I wish mine eyes
Would, with themselves, shut up my thoughts.[1] I find
They are inclined to do so.
Sebastian: Please you, sir,
Do not omit the heavy offer of it.[2]
It seldom visits sorrow; when it doth,
It is a comforter.
Antonio: We two, my lord,
Will guard your person while you take your rest …

[1] *I wish that closing my eyes would also interrupt my thoughts*
[2] *do not miss the opportunity to benefit from a deep sleep*

The King quickly falls asleep, and Ariel slips away.

Antonio and Sebastian are puzzled; they both feel wide awake, while all their fellows have fallen into a deep sleep. Antonio, hesitant at first, puts a suggestion to his friend:

Antonio: What might,
            Worthy Sebastian, O, what might – ? No more;
            And yet, methinks I see it in thy face
            What thou shouldst be. Th'occasion speaks thee,[1] and
            My strong imagination sees a crown
            Dropping upon thy head.

    [1] *this opportunity calls on you to take action*

Sebastian responds cautiously. Perhaps Antonio is talking in his sleep, he suggests lightly. On the contrary, says Antonio; it is Sebastian who is deliberately shutting his eyes.

The two men continue to talk obliquely, circling around the idea which Antonio has raised. Antonio gradually comes to the point:

Antonio: Will you grant with me
            That Ferdinand is drowned?
Sebastian: He's gone.
Antonio: Then tell me,
            Who's the next heir of Naples?
Sebastian: Claribel.
Antonio: She that is Queen of Tunis; she that dwells
            Ten leagues beyond man's life [1] ...

    [1] *more than a lifetime's journey away*

Sebastian claims not to understand what his friend is implying. Antonio goes further: the King's daughter is now so far away, he suggests, that she can scarcely be considered heir to the throne of Naples.

Antonio brings Sebastian's attention to the sleeping bodies on the ground:

Antonio: Say this were death
That now hath seized them; why, they were[1] no worse
Than now they are. There be[2] that can rule Naples
As well as he that sleeps[3] …

[1] *would be*
[2] *there are those*
[3] *the King*

Sebastian remembers that Antonio, now Duke of Milan, gained his position of power by removing his brother, Prospero. He asks Antonio whether his conscience is troubled; Antonio shrugs off the question impatiently. The thought has never occurred to him.

The action required to make Sebastian King of Naples will be simple and quick; Antonio will kill Alonso, and Sebastian will do the same to Gonzalo, who could prove troublesome if allowed to live. The other courtiers will easily be persuaded to accept whatever version of events they are given.

Sebastian's mind is made up. He will follow his friend's example and seize power for himself. As a reward, Antonio will be freed from the levy which he has been paying Alonso since they first agreed to expel Prospero:

Sebastian: As thou got'st Milan,
I'll come by Naples. Draw thy sword! One stroke
Shall free thee from the tribute which thou payest,
And I the king shall love thee.
Antonio: Draw together,
And when I rear my hand, do you the like
To fall it on Gonzalo.[1]

[1] *when I raise my hand, you do the same and*
bring your sword down on Gonzalo

A narrow escape

As the two of them are conferring, Ariel arrives on the scene. Prospero has sent him; he has become aware of the danger facing Gonzalo, the man who treated him kindly when he was cast out to sea all those years ago. It is also essential to Prospero's plan that Ferdinand's father Alonso remains King of Naples.

The invisible spirit sings in Gonzalo's ear, warning him of the treachery that is about to take place. Just as Sebastian and Antonio are about to strike, Gonzalo wakes with a start, and his shouting wakes the King. They are horrified to see the two men standing above them, fearsome expressions on their faces, with swords drawn.

Sebastian hastily invents an explanation. They have drawn their weapons, he claims, because they have just heard a terrible noise, probably the bellowing of a herd of wild animals. Antonio backs up his story, but Gonzalo is unsure:

Antonio: O, 'twas a din to fright a monster's ear –
To make an earthquake! Sure it was the roar
Of a whole herd of lions.
Alonso: Heard you this, Gonzalo?
Gonzalo: Upon mine honour, sir, I heard a humming,
And that a strange one too, which did awake me.

There is clearly danger on the island. The King decides that they should move on and continue the search for Ferdinand.

More survivors

Caliban is unhappily going about his task of collecting firewood, as instructed by Prospero. He curses his master, who torments him for the slightest misdemeanour. Prospero's spirits are everywhere, and can take on a multitude of forms:

Caliban: … For every trifle are they set upon me:
Sometime like apes that mow[1] and chatter at me
And after bite me, then like hedgehogs which
Lie tumbling in my barefoot way and mount
Their pricks at my footfall. Sometime am I
All wound[2] with adders, who with cloven[3] tongues
Do hiss me into madness.

[1] *grimace*
[2] *entwined, wrapped around*
[3] *split, forked*

Suddenly, Caliban sees a human form approaching. Believing it to be another of Prospero's spirits, sent to punish him for working too slowly, he tries to hide by lying stock-still on the ground.

The visitor is Trinculo, the King's jester, another survivor from the shipwreck. Dark clouds are gathering again, and he is looking for shelter, afraid that the terrible storm that destroyed their vessel is about to return.

Trinculo sees Caliban on the ground, half-covered by a long, rough cloak. He is puzzled by the strange being. His first thought is that, in the right circumstances, he could make money from the creature:

Trinculo: What have we here, a man or a fish? Dead or alive? ... Were I in England now (as once I was) and had but this fish painted,[1] not a holiday fool there but would give a piece of silver [2] ... When they will not give a doit [3] to relieve a lame beggar, they will lay out ten to see a dead Indian.[4]

[1] *painted on a sign (for example, outside a booth at a fairground)*
[2] *every gullible holidaymaker would pay good money to see the attraction*
[3] *small coin of very little value*
[4] *an exotic sideshow such as the preserved body of a native American*

... they will lay out ten to see a dead Indian.

Many European travellers to the New World of the Americas brought indigenous people back with them, often as objects of curiosity for public exhibition. The explorer Martin Frobisher, for example, brought back a number of Inuit people in the 1570s following his voyages to find the 'Northwest passage', a route through the Arctic Sea north of Canada which would make it easier for European traders to reach China, India and the East Indies.

The arrival of the Inuit aroused enormous interest, and many descriptions and paintings of them were produced. The unfortunate Inuit rarely lived long after capture, often succumbing to diseases caught from their captors.

Examining Caliban more closely, Trinculo decides that the strange, motionless animal is not a fish, but an inhabitant of the island who has been struck by lightning. Either way, he needs to take shelter:

> *Trinculo:* Alas, the storm is come again. My best way is to creep under his gaberdine;[1] there is no other shelter hereabout. Misery acquaints a man with strange bedfellows!
>
> [1] *long, loose cloak*

Another of the ship's passengers now wanders onto the scene. It is Stephano, the King's butler, with a bottle in his hand, singing drunkenly. Caliban, assuming this is yet another of Prospero's spirits, begs for mercy.

Stephano, hearing Caliban's cries, looks down at the source of the noise. When he sees all the limbs sticking out from under the cloak, he believes he has stumbled upon a four-legged monster. Presumably the monster, who is trembling, has cried out because he is unwell; Stephano wonders, in his befuddled state, how the monster came to speak the same language as him. Like Trinculo, he sees an opportunity to profit from this strange creature:

> *Stephano:* This is some monster of the isle, with four legs, who hath got, as I take it, an ague.[1] Where the devil should he learn our language? ... If I can recover[2] him and keep him tame, and get to Naples with him, he's a present for any emperor ...
>
> [1] *illness, fever*
> [2] *revive*

What the monster needs, decides Stephano, is a drink. Caliban is fearful, but Stephano manages to pour some of the wine from his bottle into the creature's mouth.

The 'salvage man' – a wild, uncivilized creature, often emerging from the depths of the forest – was a recurrent figure in medieval folklore throughout Europe.

The idea persisted into the Renaissance, and the character plays an important role in *The Faerie Queene*, an epic poem of 1596 dedicated to Elizabeth I, which was immensely popular in Shakespeare's time.

"Caliban may be a 'salvage man', but as The Tempest *unfolds, he proves to be more rational and sympathetic than the two Neapolitan conspirators or the two drunken servants who represent European culture's corrupt underside."*

Virginia Mason and Alden T. Vaughan, Introduction to the Arden edition of *The Tempest*, 1999

Trinculo, recognizing Stephano's voice, is terrified. His friend, like everyone else, surely drowned in the shipwreck; it must be an evil spirit that he can hear, and he cries out in distress. Stephano, in turn, is now amazed:

Stephano: Four legs and two voices – a most delicate[1] monster!

[1] *delightful*

However, when the monster's second voice calls out his name, Stephano is shaken, and decides to abandon the sinister creature. At this point the two men finally realise the truth: they have both survived the storm. Stephano pulls Trinculo out from under the cloak. The jester dances around excitedly, but Stephano is queasy and not inclined to move too quickly:

Trinculo: And art thou living, Stephano? O Stephano, two Neapolitans 'scaped?
Stephano: Prithee, do not turn me about; my stomach is not constant.[1]

[1] *stable, steady*

A new master for Caliban

Caliban, observing their behaviour, is enthralled by these two beings. They are not spirits, he decides; in fact, one of them is surely a divinity to be worshipped:

> Caliban: These be fine things, an if they be not sprites;[1]
> That's a brave god and bears celestial liquor.
> I will kneel to him.

> [1] *if they aren't spirits*

Stephano and Trinculo discuss their escape from the shipwreck. Trinculo managed to swim ashore, while Stephano saved himself by clinging on to a barrel of wine thrown from the ship; the barrel is now safely hidden in a cave near the beach.

The two men find Caliban amusing: far from being a monster, they decide, he is a harmless and comical creature, particularly now that the repeated swigs from Stephano's bottle are taking effect.

> *"Caliban is malicious, cowardly, false, and base in his inclinations; and yet he is essentially different from the vulgar knaves of a civilized world ... he never falls into the prosaic and low familiarity of his drunken associates, for he is a poetical being in his way; he always speaks in verse."*
>
> August Wilhelm Schlegel, *Lectures on Dramatic Art and Literature*, 1809

Caliban, meanwhile, becomes more and more effusive about his new masters. When Stephano claims to be the man in the moon, Caliban believes him without question. He volunteers to desert Prospero and serve Stephano instead:

> *Caliban:*　I'll show thee the best springs; I'll pluck thee berries;
> I'll fish for thee, and get thee wood enough.
> A plague upon the tyrant that I serve!

Stephano is delighted; since all the others on the King's ship must have perished in the storm, he and Trinculo, with this creature's help, can take possession of the entire island. He offers Caliban the bottle yet again, and his new devotee, singing exuberantly, leads the men off to explore the island.

Young love   III, i

Ferdinand has been set to work by Prospero, and is busy carrying heavy logs from one place to another. The work is menial and hard, but the young man presses on without complaining, sustained by his love for Miranda:

> *Ferdinand:*　　　　　　　　　This my mean task
> Would be as heavy to me as odious,[1] but
> The mistress which I serve quickens what's dead,[2]
> And makes my labours pleasures. O, she is
> Ten times more gentle than her father's crabbed[3] ...

> [1]　*as disheartening as it is detestable*
> [2]　*were it not for the fact that Miranda brings everything to life*
> [3]　*disagreeable, irritable*

Miranda now comes to talk to her beloved. Prospero, unseen, secretly observes the pair from a distance. His daughter is worried that Ferdinand is working too hard; her father is occupied with his studies for the next few hours, she says, so Ferdinand should rest for a while. She even volunteers to take over the work herself.

Ferdinand refuses to stop. His devotion to Prospero's daughter drives him on, and he is undaunted by the gruelling task he has been given. For the first time he asks her name; she tells him, even though it is against her father's command.

Ferdinand: Admired Miranda!
Indeed the top of admiration,[1] worth
What's dearest to the world!
                    … For several virtues
Have I liked several women; never any
With so full soul but some defect in her
Did quarrel with the noblest grace she owed[2]
And put it to the foil.[3] But you, O you,
So perfect and so peerless, are created
Of every creature's best.

[1] *the epitome of wonder; the most worthy*
    of being admired
[2] *possessed*
[3] *defeated it, thwarted it*

Miranda, too, declares that Ferdinand is the only man in the world she will ever love. Putting aside her feelings of shyness and restraint, she addresses him directly:

Miranda: Hence, bashful cunning,[1]
And prompt[2] me, plain and holy innocence!
I am your wife, if you will marry me;
If not, I'll die your maid. To be your fellow
You may deny me, but I'll be your servant
Whether you will or no.

[1] *no more coyness*
[2] *guide*

Holding hands, the two of them pledge their betrothal. Prospero, watching benevolently, is gladdened by the depth and tenderness of their love. However, there is more to be done before his plan comes to fruition, and he sets off back to his books.

A revolution is planned

Stephano, Trinculo and Caliban are still wandering around the island, squabbling drunkenly. Caliban has explained to them that there are only two other inhabitants, Prospero and Miranda. As Stephano addresses Caliban, the jester Trinculo cannot help feeling doubtful about the nation they intend to govern:

Stephano: ... Servant monster, drink to me.

Trinculo: Servant monster? The folly of this island! They say there's but five upon this isle; we are three of them. If th'other two be brained like us, the state totters.

Caliban is still devoted to the butler Stephano, who plies him constantly with drink. However, he has taken against Trinculo, believing him to be a coward. Trinculo is outraged that a creature like Caliban should insult him, and the two of them argue raucously.

Stephano, the self-appointed ruler of the island, issues a stern warning:

Stephano: Trinculo, keep a good tongue in your head. If you prove a mutineer – the next tree! [1] The poor monster's my subject, and he shall not suffer indignity.

Caliban: I thank my noble lord.

[1] *you'll be hanged*

Caliban reminds his master that he has a request to make, and Stephano agrees to listen. At this point, the invisible Ariel joins the three of them. As Caliban starts describing his grievances against Prospero, Ariel interrupts: imitating Trinculo's voice, he accuses Caliban of lying.

Stephano and Caliban turn angrily on the jester, who indignantly denies having said anything. Caliban continues with his appeal to Stephano. He wants to be free from Prospero forever:

Caliban: I say, by sorcery he got this isle.
From me he got it. If thy greatness[1] will
Revenge it on him …
Stephano: How now shall this be compassed?[2] Canst thou
bring me to the party?[3]
Caliban: Yea, yea, my lord, I'll yield[4] him thee asleep,
Where thou mayst knock a nail into his head.

[1] *your highness, your majesty*
[2] *accomplished, managed* •
[3] *the person in question*
[4] *deliver, show*

Ariel, again imitating Trinculo, accuses first Caliban and then Stephano of lying. Losing patience, Stephano strikes his companion, to Caliban's delight. The jester sullenly moves away, blaming the wine for Stephano's mindless belligerence:

Trinculo: A pox o'your bottle! This can sack and drinking do.[1]
A murrain[2] on your monster …

[1] *this is what wine and drunkenness can lead to*
[2] *plague*

Caliban now describes his plan in more detail. He proposes to take Stephano to Prospero's dwelling-place; the old man usually sleeps in the afternoon, he explains. Before putting Prospero to death, Caliban emphasises, they must destroy his books, which are the source of his power:

Caliban: ... 'tis a custom with him
I'th' afternoon to sleep. There thou mayst brain him,
Having first seized his books, or with a log
Batter his skull, or paunch him[1] with a stake,
Or cut his wezand[2] with thy knife. Remember
First to possess his books, for without them
He's but a sot,[3] as I am, nor hath not
One spirit to command.

[1] *stab him in the belly*
[2] *windpipe*
[3] *useless fool*

Remember
First to possess his books ...

"Caliban understands the power of the book: as fashioners of modern coups d'état *begin by seizing the television station, so he reiterates the need to begin by possessing the books."*

Jonathan Bate, *Soul of the Age*, 2008

Prospero's daughter provides a further incentive for the planned assassination:

Caliban:	I never saw a woman
	But only Sycorax, my dam,[1] and she;
	But she as far surpasseth Sycorax
	As great'st does least.
Stephano:	Is it so brave a lass?
Caliban:	Ay, lord, she will become[2] thy bed, I warrant,
	And bring thee forth brave brood.
Stephano:	Monster, I will kill this man. His daughter and I
	will be king and queen – save our graces! – and
	Trinculo and thyself shall be viceroys.

[1] *except for Sycorax, my mother*
[2] *be suitable for*

Within half an hour, Caliban affirms, Prospero will be asleep. The three companions, excited at their prospects, are reconciled, and they start singing cheerfully.

Suddenly music is heard accompanying their song, stopping them in their tracks. It is Ariel, unseen, playing a pipe and drum. Trinculo is terrified; at first, Stephano shouts defiantly at the invisible source of the sound, but then he too pleads for mercy. Caliban reassures them:

Caliban:	Be not afeard. The isle is full of noises,
	Sounds and sweet airs that give delight and hurt not.
	Sometimes a thousand twangling instruments
	Will hum about mine ears; and sometimes voices,
	That if I then had waked after long sleep,
	Will make me sleep again; and then in dreaming,
	The clouds, methought, would open and show riches
	Ready to drop upon me, that[1] when I waked
	I cried to dream again.

[1] *so that*

As the music moves away, Trinculo and Stephano, fascinated, decide to follow it, taking Caliban with them. Finally, Ariel slips away to warn his master of the plot.

... Sounds and sweet airs that give delight ...

In 1596, James Burbage, carpenter, actor and theatrical entrepreneur, invested a huge sum of money in a new theatre. The property, which had once been part of the Blackfriars monastery, was in a fashionable, wealthy area in the heart of London. Burbage was convinced that a venue of this kind would be far more profitable than the open-air theatres of the time, which had many disadvantages: they were generally in muddy sites at the fringes of the city, had a reputation for rowdiness, and were unusable during the winter months.

However, Burbage's venture was a disaster. Local residents successfully petitioned the government, demanding that the property must not be used as a theatre:

"It will grow to be a very great annoyance and trouble, not only to all the noblemen and gentlemen thereabout inhabiting but allso a generall inconvenience to all the inhabitants ... by reason of the great resort and gathering together of all manner of vagrant and lewde persons that, under cullor of resorting to the players, will come thither and worke all manner of mischeefe ..."

Burbage died the following year, leaving the theatre to his son Richard, one of Shakespeare's partners in the King's Men theatre company. For more than ten years, the building was empty, or was leased out to other tenants. However, in 1608, the King's Men finally gained permission to use the Blackfriars.

This new indoor theatre, with its intimate, candlelit atmosphere and subtle acoustics, opened up a whole new world of possibilities, which Shakespeare was quick to exploit in his later plays such as *The Tempest:*

"... the Blackfriars stayed open. It would see the last great phase of the poet's career, when his final masterpieces were written with the indoor theatre in mind, with the magical effects in music, lighting and staging that it offered."

Michael Wood, *In Search of Shakespeare*, 2003

A captivating vision

King Alonso and his companions are still wandering around the island in the hope of finding Ferdinand. The King's elderly adviser Gonzalo is exhausted, and asks if they can pause for a rest. The King is also weary; anyway, he concludes, their attempt to find his missing son is futile. He finally accepts that Ferdinand was drowned in the shipwreck. It is time to give up the search.

Antonio reminds the King's brother of their plan; they must not be deterred, he insists, by the failure of their first attempt to assassinate the King. He is adamant that it must be done this evening, while their victims are still tired from their long hours of searching. Sebastian agrees: the planned assassination must go ahead.

Suddenly the air is filled with beautiful, strange music. At the same time Prospero arrives, unseen, and watches proceedings from a vantage point above the royal party.

The men look on in amazement as a group of strangely-shaped beings bring in a table laden with food. Bowing and gesturing gracefully, they wordlessly invite the King and his companions to eat, then they depart.

The men can hardly believe their eyes. Perhaps all those travellers' tales of unicorns and other exotic creatures are true? Gonzalo considers how difficult it would be to convince people at home of what they have just witnessed:

Gonzalo: If in Naples
I should report this now, would they believe me?
If I should say I saw such islanders
(For certes,[1] these are people of the island),
Who, though they are of monstrous[2] shape, yet note
Their manners are more gentle, kind, than of
Our human generation[3] you shall find
Many – nay, almost any.

Prospero: [*aside*] Honest lord,
                Thou hast said well, for some of you there present
                Are worse than devils.

> 1 *certainly*
> 2 *bizarre, unearthly*
> 3 *our species*

At first, the King is reluctant to taste the feast that has
been laid out in front of them. He eventually agrees; even
if the food has been poisoned, he reflects sadly, he has
little to lose. He invites Sebastian and Antonio to join him:

Alonso: I will stand to[1] and feed,
                Although my last;[2] no matter, since I feel
                The best is past. Brother, my lord the Duke,
                Stand to and do as we.

> 1 *come forward*
> 2 *even if it is my last meal*

Past crimes are remembered

Just as the men are about to start eating, there is a flash
of lightning and a deafening thunderclap. Ariel appears,
in the form of a harpy, a monstrous bird of prey with a
woman's face. The beast flaps its wings, and the banquet
suddenly vanishes.

Ariel addresses the three men standing at the bare table.
They find themselves unable to lift their swords, and he
mocks their attempts to fight him off:

Ariel: You fools! I and my fellows
                Are ministers of fate. The elements
                Of whom your swords are tempered may as well
                Wound the loud winds ...
                                      ... If you could hurt,
                Your swords are now too massy[1] for your strengths
                And will not be uplifted.

> 1 *heavy*

They have brought about their present suffering, declares Ariel, by their evil actions:

> *Ariel:*   ... you three
> From Milan did supplant good Prospero,
> Exposed unto the sea, which hath requit [1] it,
> Him and his innocent child; for which foul deed,
> The powers delaying, not forgetting, have
> Incensed the seas and shores – yea, all the creatures –
> Against your peace. Thee of thy son, Alonso,
> They have bereft [2] ...
>
> [1] *repaid, avenged*
> [2] *deprived*

Their only hope of escaping a life of anguish on this deserted island, he warns, is heartfelt repentance and an honest life in the future. There is another thunderclap, and Ariel vanishes. The strange beings who first brought in the banquet now return and remove the empty table; this time, their gestures are mocking and scornful.

Prospero congratulates his servant Ariel. As a result of his skill, and Prospero's own magical powers, Alonso, Sebastian and Antonio are all under his control:

> *Prospero:*   My high charms work,
> And these, mine enemies, are all knit up
> In their distractions. [1] They now are in my power ...
>
> [1] *entangled by their temporary insanity*

Gonzalo, who has not heard Ariel's denunciation, is alarmed to see the three men standing, shocked and bewildered, gazing into space.

The King is almost overcome with remorse, and he now sets off to find his son, even if he is at the bottom of the ocean. Sebastian and Antonio, by contrast, resolve to find the spirits who have been taunting them and fight them one by one.

Gonzalo concludes that, all these years after the overthrow of Prospero, the men's consciences have finally started to catch up with them:

> Gonzalo: All three of them are desperate: their great guilt,
> Like poison given to work a great time after,
> Now 'gins to bite the spirits.

He asks his younger companions to follow the men and keep them from harm; all three of them, he believes, are in a dangerous state of mind.

Prospero gives his blessing IV, i

Ferdinand's arduous physical task is now over. Prospero explains that he was testing the young man before agreeing to his marriage to Miranda:

> Prospero: If I have too austerely punished you,
> Your compensation makes amends, for I
> Have given you here a third of mine own life [1] ...
> ... All thy vexations
> Were but my trials of thy love, and thou
> Hast strangely [2] stood the test.

> [1] *many years of my life; one of my greatest riches*
> [2] *exceptionally*

Prospero is now happy for the two of them to wed. However, he gives Ferdinand a stern warning that, until that day comes, they must remain chaste:

> Prospero: ... If thou dost break her virgin-knot before
> All sanctimonious [1] ceremonies may
> With full and holy rite be ministered,
> No sweet aspersion [2] shall the heavens let fall
> To make this contract grow; but barren hate,
> Sour-eyed disdain and discord shall bestrew
> The union of your bed ...

> [1] *sanctified, holy*
> [2] *grace, blessings*

Ferdinand assures Prospero that he respects the sanctity of marriage, and will not give in to temptation. Prospero is satisfied, and asks him to sit down next to his beloved.

Prospero now calls for Ariel. He and his fellow spirits carried out their previous task admirably, says Prospero; now he has another assignment for them, a pleasant, magical display for the benefit of Miranda and Ferdinand.

In 1613, lavish festivities were held at the court of King James I to celebrate the marriage of the King's daughter, Princess Elizabeth. Events included fourteen plays, six of which were by Shakespeare. *The Tempest* – already played before the King two years earlier – was one of these. Some scholars believe that Shakespeare added a specially-written masque to the original version of *The Tempest* with the royal wedding in mind, and that this adapted version is the play we know today.

Masques – elaborate musical and visual entertainments, often with themes drawn from mythology – were hugely popular at King James's court. Courtiers and members of the royal family often joined the professionals in the performances:

"Masques were the original multimedia event ... Staged at great expense for special court occasions – weddings, birthdays, investitures – masques treated the audience to a vision of court ladies and gentlemen dressed in lavish costumes within spectacular moving sets."

Virginia Mason and Alden T. Vaughan, Introduction to the Arden edition of *The Tempest*, 1999

While Ariel sets about his work, Prospero reminds Ferdinand – now seated next to Miranda – of the promise he has just made:

Prospero: Look thou be true. Do not give dalliance [1]
Too much the rein.[2] The strongest oaths are straw
To th' fire i'th' blood. Be more abstemious …

[1] *flirtation, intimacy*
[2] *too much freedom*

Prospero urges Ariel to hurry up with the show. As soft music starts to play, he commands the audience of the two lovers to remain silent.

Three goddesses come down to earth

The first spirit to appear in Prospero's masque is Iris, rainbow goddess and messenger of the heavens. Her message is for Ceres, goddess of agriculture and the harvest. The queen of the heavens herself, Juno, wife of Jupiter and goddess of marriage, has sent for her; their encounter is to take place down here on earth.

Iris: Ceres, most bounteous lady, thy rich leas [1]
Of wheat, rye, barley, vetches,[2] oats and peas;
Thy turfy mountains where live nibbling sheep …
… the queen o'th' sky,
Whose watery arch and messenger am I,
Bids thee leave these, and with her sovereign grace,[3]
Here on this grass-plot, in this very place,
To come and sport.

[1] *fields, meadows*
[2] *crops grown as fodder for animals*
[3] *her majesty*

Ceres arrives, and Iris explains that Juno has summoned her to celebrate a marriage-contract. Ceres is concerned that Venus and her son Cupid may be with Juno; since the two of them helped Pluto, god of the underworld, to steal her daughter, Ceres has sworn to shun their company.

Iris reassures her that she is safe from the lustful Venus and her troublesome boy; their best efforts to influence the young couple here on the island failed, and they have made their way home to Cyprus.

Juno now comes down to earth, and she and Ceres sing together, promising happiness and prosperity to the betrothed couple:

Juno:	Honour, riches, marriage-blessing,
	Long continuance and increasing,[1]
	Hourly joys be still[2] upon you;
	Juno sings her blessings on you.
Ceres:	Earth's increase, foison[3] plenty,
	Barns and garners[4] never empty.
	Vines with clustering bunches growing,
	Plants with goodly burden bowing ...

[1] *long life and fruitfulness*
[2] *always*
[3] *abundance*
[4] *granaries, stores*

Ferdinand is enthralled by the display, and amazed at Prospero's ability to call upon the island's spirits. He remarks that he would happily spend the rest of his life on the island.

The masque continues. Now Iris calls for the water-nymphs to leave their streams and join the celebrations. To accompany them, she summons the reapers from their fields:

Iris: You sunburned sicklemen, of August weary,
               Come hither from the furrow and be merry;
               Make holiday! Your rye-straw hats put on,
               And these fresh nymphs encounter[1] every one
               In country footing.[2]

[1] *join, take a partner*
[2] *rustic dancing*

The water-nymphs and harvesters dance; but before their dance is over, Prospero jumps up in alarm. He has suddenly remembered the plot to take his life, reported to him by Ariel earlier in the day. Caliban, Stephano and Trinculo are no doubt on their way, with murderous intentions, at this very minute.

Prospero hurriedly orders the various spirits away. The performance is over. Ferdinand and Miranda are shocked at the sudden change that has come over Prospero, and the untimely ending of the entertainment.

Although Shakespeare was very familiar with the conventions of the courtly masque, the abrupt and chaotic end of Prospero's display suggests that the author had his doubts about this notoriously sycophantic form of entertainment:

"Shakespeare, shockingly, punctuates the entire enterprise by bringing the masque to a sudden halt ... Prospero, who has been absorbed in his artistic creation, terminates the masque after realising that he has been so distracted ... Real-world plots expose the masque's propensity for self-absorption and self-celebration."

James Shapiro, *1606: William Shakespeare and the Year of Lear*, 2015

Noticing Ferdinand's dismay, Prospero tries to reassure him; the masque, like everything else, must eventually come to an end.

Prospero: Be cheerful, sir.
Our revels are now ended. These our actors,
As I foretold you, were all spirits and
Are melted into air, into thin air;
And – like the baseless fabric of this vision[1] –
The cloud-capped towers, the gorgeous palaces,
The solemn temples, the great globe itself,
Yea, all which it inherit,[2] shall dissolve,
And like this insubstantial pageant faded,
Leave not a rack[3] behind. We are such stuff
As dreams are made on, and our little life
Is rounded with a sleep.

[1] *like this spectacle, which had no foundation in reality*
[2] *occupy it, possess it*
[3] *cloud, trace*

"*In* The Tempest *Shakespeare achieved what some competent critics regard as his final and greatest play. In its poetry he reached the farthest limits possible to the English language in expression and solemn music. The thought is still packed, but no longer obscure, the verse free but perfectly controlled ... In the later speeches he reached his final mastery over words. The meaning is clear, the thought deep, the emotional music perfect ... until the English language in its turn has perished, in* The Tempest *lies its greatest achievement.*"

G. B. Harrison, *Introducing Shakespeare*, 1966

An assassin approaches

Apologising for his agitated state of mind, Prospero asks Ferdinand and Miranda to withdraw into his room and leave him on his own for a while.

When they have gone, Prospero summons Ariel and asks for the latest news about the conspirators. The spirit describes how the three of them, drunk and aggressive, were stopped in their tracks by the music played by the invisible Ariel. They proceeded to follow the music, like calves following their mother's mooing, wherever it led them:

> *Ariel:*   … I charmed their ears
> That calf-like they my lowing followed, through
> Toothed briars, sharp furzes, pricking gorse and thorns,
> Which entered their frail shins. At last I left them
> I'th' filthy-mantled[1] pool beyond your cell …
>
> [1] *slime-covered*

Prospero is pleased with Ariel. He now asks his servant to fetch some of his fine clothes and regalia, and to hang them out to attract the conspirators' attention. He reflects angrily on Caliban's wickedness and ingratitude:

> *Prospero:* A devil, a born devil, on whose nature
> Nurture can never stick;[1] on whom my pains
> Humanely taken – all, all lost, quite lost!
>
> [1] *education and enlightenment can never take hold*

Prospero and Ariel now stand aside: Caliban is approaching. He is followed by Stephano and Trinculo, who are soaking, filthy and bad-tempered. They have found themselves dragged through thorn-bushes and dumped in a foul, muddy pond; to make matters worse, they have lost their wine.

Stephano is about to go back and attempt to recover his bottle from the pond, but Caliban urges him to act:

Caliban: Prithee, my king, be quiet. Seest thou here;
              This is the mouth o'th' cell. No noise, and enter.
              Do that good mischief which may make this island
              Thine own forever, and I, thy Caliban,
              For aye thy foot-licker.[1]
Stephano: Give me thy hand. I do begin to have bloody thoughts.

    [1] *your servant for ever*

At this moment the jester Trinculo notices the gaudy clothes hanging near Prospero's cell. This finery is fit for a king, he tells his companion excitedly.

Caliban furiously tells Trinculo to ignore the robes; he is wasting time. However, Stephano too has become interested in the clothes. To Caliban's exasperation, the men start arguing over who should own which garments.

Stephano: Put off that gown, Trinculo. By this hand, I'll have
              that gown.
Trinculo: Thy grace shall have it.
Caliban: The dropsy[1] drown this fool! What do you mean
              To dote thus on such luggage?[2] Let't alone
              And do the murder first.

    [1] *disease in which the body becomes bloated*
       with fluid
    [2] *useless items, trappings*

If Prospero wakes, warns Caliban, they will be in serious trouble. Stephano tells him to stop complaining, and orders him to carry some of the clothes; he aims to take them back to the cave where he has hidden his barrel of wine.

While Stephano and Trinculo are busy piling more and more clothes onto Caliban, there is a sudden uproar: a pack of hounds appears and sets upon the three of them. It is the work of Prospero and Ariel, who have conjured up spirits in the form of hunting-dogs. They urge the creatures to chase the three conspirators, who flee in terror.

Prospero tells Ariel to ensure that, as well as being hunted by dogs, the men are tormented by pinches, cramps and convulsions. He assures the spirit that his work is nearly over:

Prospero: At this hour
            Lies at my mercy all mine enemies.
            Shortly shall all my labours end, and thou
            Shalt have the air at freedom.[1]

            [1] will be able to take to the air at liberty

A farewell to magic   V, i

Prospero, now wearing his magician's robe, is confident that things are progressing as they should:

Prospero: Now does my project gather to a head.[1]
            My charms crack not;[2] my spirits obey; and time
            Goes upright with his carriage.[3]

            [1] come to the boil; reach its culmination
            [2] do not fail
            [3] the burden of time is no longer heavy

He asks Ariel for the latest news of the King and his companions. The spirit informs him that Alonso, Sebastian and Antonio are still in the state of temporary insanity that overcame them when, in the guise of a harpy, he denounced them for their crimes. As instructed, Ariel has confined them to a nearby grove of trees.

Gonzalo and the other courtiers are heartbroken at their fellows' suffering. They make a pitiful spectacle:

Ariel: Your charm so strongly works 'em[1]
            That, if you now beheld them, your affections
            Would become tender.
Prospero: Dost thou think so, spirit?
Ariel: Mine would, sir, were I human.

            [1] works upon them, affects them

Ariel is right, reflects Prospero; it is fitting for him, as a human being, to feel compassion for the men's anguish. He decides that the time has come to forgive past misdeeds and restore harmony. The men are clearly repentant, and their punishment will go on no longer:

Prospero: Though with their high wrongs I am struck to th' quick,[1]
Yet with my nobler reason 'gainst my fury
Do I take part.[2] The rarer action is
In virtue than in vengeance.[3] They being penitent,
The sole drift of my purpose doth extend
Not a frown further.[4] Go, release them, Ariel.
My charms I'll break; their senses I'll restore;
And they shall be themselves.

[1] *their terrible crimes have wounded me*
[2] *take sides, ally myself*
[3] *virtue is a nobler basis for action than revenge*
[4] *my overriding aim has been achieved, and my hostile intentions have come to an end*

---

*... The rarer action is
In virtue than in vengeance.*

In Shakespeare's time, revenge was a hotly debated issue. The settling of scores through violent action outside the law, although frowned on by the authorities, was widespread.

Prospero's decision not to take further vengeance echoes the thoughts of one of Shakespeare's contemporaries, the philosopher and statesman Francis Bacon:

"Revenge is a kind of wild justice; which the more man's nature runs to, the more ought law to weed it out ... in taking revenge, a man is but even with his enemy; but in passing it over, he is superior; for it is a prince's part to pardon. That which is past is gone, and irrevocable; and wise men have enough to do with things present and to come ..."

Francis Bacon, *On Revenge*, 1597

Ariel sets off on his task. Prospero now starts to trace a large circle on the ground. As he does so, he calls out to the countless spirits, fairies and elves of the island with whose help he has performed his various magical tasks. He remembers some of the spells he has cast with their assistance:

Prospero: … I have bedimmed
The noontide sun,[1] called forth the mutinous winds,
And 'twixt the green sea and the azured vault
Set roaring war[2] …
                                    … the strong-based promontory
Have I made shake, and by the spurs[3] plucked up
The pine and cedar …

[1] *caused eclipses of the sun*
[2] *created tempestuous war between the sea*
     and the sky
[3] *roots*

Now, however, the time for magic is over. With one final command for solemn music to sound from the heavens, he relinquishes his supernatural powers for good:

Prospero: But this rough magic
I here abjure[1] …
                    … I'll break my staff,
Bury it certain fathoms in the earth,
And deeper than did ever plummet sound[2]
I'll drown my book.

[1] *renounce*
[2] *deeper in the ocean than any plumb-line*
     has ever measured

The Duke reappears

Ariel now returns, leading the forlorn group of men: first King Alonso, still grief-stricken and distraught, with his sorrowful attendant Gonzalo; then his brother Sebastian and Prospero's own brother Antonio, both agitated to the point of insanity, attended by their courtiers.

The men are led into the circle drawn by Prospero, where they stand spellbound. Prospero observes them, and reflects on their actions, knowing that they are oblivious to his presence in their current state.

His eyes fill with tears as he sees Gonzalo's obvious distress, and he remembers how the old councillor helped him in his time of need. As for the others, he has not forgotten their crimes: Alonso, Sebastian and Antonio all took part in Prospero's expulsion from Milan. Sebastian and Antonio, moreover, had planned to murder the King when the opportunity arose. They are all suffering for their wrongdoings now, remarks Prospero, and will be forgiven.

Prospero is aware that the spell is starting to fade: soon the men will be conscious of their surroundings. He asks Ariel to fetch his stately clothes, and removes his magician's robe. He intends to present himself to the royal party as his true self: Prospero, Duke of Milan. As Ariel helps his master with his ceremonial garments, he looks forward to his freedom and sings joyfully:

> *Ariel:*   Where the bee sucks, there suck I,
> In a cowslip's bell I lie;
> There I couch[1] when owls do cry.
> On the bat's back I do fly
> After[2] summer merrily.
> Merrily, merrily, shall I live now,
> Under the blossom that hangs on the bough.
>
> [1] *lie, rest*
> [2] *following*

Prospero is delighted with the song. He will miss Ariel when the spirit is finally set free; but for now there is more work to do. He instructs his servant to go to the King's ship, which is now safely at anchor, and wake the sleeping crew. The spirit, still invisible, must then bring the ship's master and boatswain to join the King's party.

In the 17th century, European playwrights were becoming increasingly interested in the three 'classical unities' – supposedly set out by Aristotle – which held that a play should have a single central plot, should take place over a single day, and should happen in a single place. The idea does not seem to have appealed to Shakespeare, whose plays frequently have complex sub-plots, span long distances of time, and jump freely from one location to another. *The Tempest* is exceptional among his plays in that it observes these 'rules' remarkably closely.

Shakespeare's friend and rival Ben Jonson, who had a strong grounding in the literature of ancient Greece and Rome, was a great believer in the classical unities. However, the notoriously opinionated and argumentative Jonson was not easily pleased. He was clearly vexed by the popularity of *The Tempest*, believing that a play's language, characters and plot should all be based firmly in the real world.

"In The Tempest, *Shakespeare finally fulfilled Ben Jonson's highest aspirations. The play observes the classical unities of time, place, and action. Not that he was given much credit for it by Ben, who, in his Induction to* Bartholomew Fair *of 1614, refers scathingly to 'a servant-monster' and to 'Tales, Tempests and such like drolleries'."*

Nicholas Fogg, *Hidden Shakespeare*, 2013

Awakening

The men in Prospero's circle gradually start to recover their senses. At first they are bewildered, and unsure whether they are in the real world or not. Prospero assures Alonso that what he sees is no illusion, and embraces him warmly:

> *Prospero:*   Behold, sir King,
> The wronged Duke of Milan, Prospero!
> For more assurance that a living prince
> Does now speak to thee, I embrace thy body,
> And to thee and thy company I bid
> A hearty welcome.

The King, feeling calmer now, is curious to know more of Prospero's story. But first he makes one thing clear: Prospero is indeed Duke of Milan. His city is now free and independent, no longer subordinate to Naples. Alonso then asks Prospero's forgiveness for his part in ousting him from his rightful Dukedom.

Prospero turns next to the elderly Gonzalo, praising him for his nobility and worthiness. Then he takes Sebastian and Antonio aside and warns them that he knows of their earlier plot to kill the King. However, he will not reveal their guilt for the time being:

> *Prospero:*   … were I so minded,
> I here could pluck his highness' frown[1] upon you
> And justify[2] you traitors! At this time
> I will tell no tales.

> [1] *bring down the King's displeasure*
> [2] *prove, establish*

Sebastian tells Antonio that it is the devil speaking, but Prospero contradicts him. He then offers his forgiveness to Antonio – whom he can hardly bring himself to call his brother – and informs him, tersely, that the Dukedom has now been restored to its rightful holder.

Alonso is keen to ask Prospero about his perilous journey to the island, but as he does so he is reminded of the loss of his son:

Alonso: Give us particulars of thy preservation,
How thou hast met us here, whom three hours since
Were wrecked upon this shore, where I have lost
(How sharp the point of this remembrance is!)
My dear son Ferdinand.

Prospero offers his sympathy, and tells the King that he must be patient and stoical. He reveals, to Alonso's amazement, that he has had the same experience himself; he lost his daughter in the same tempest.

Looking around, Prospero realises that the King's attendants are still in a state of bewilderment, unsure whether to believe their eyes. He assures them, once again, that he is the true Duke of Milan, banished from his city many years ago and abandoned on the high seas.

Welcoming Alonso once more to his own humble kingdom, Prospero takes him towards his simple dwelling-place. He promises to show the King something that will delight him:

Prospero: Welcome, sir.
This cell's my court; here have I few attendants,
And subjects none abroad.[1] Pray you, look in.
My dukedom since you have given me again,
I will requite[2] you with as good a thing …

[1]   *no subjects elsewhere*
[2]   *repay*

A joyful reunion

Prospero now approaches his cell. Pulling back the curtain, he reveals its occupants, Ferdinand and Miranda, to the King and his companions. The two young lovers are playing chess. Unaware of their audience, Miranda playfully accuses her beloved of cheating; Ferdinand denies the charge with mock indignation.

At first, Alonso is fearful that this might be yet another of the island's illusions. Then the young couple become aware of the onlookers, and hurry out to greet them. Ferdinand and his father embrace affectionately. Miranda is almost speechless, lost in admiration at the sight of so many other human beings:

Miranda: O wonder!
How many goodly creatures are there here!
How beauteous mankind is! O brave new world,
That has such people in't!
Prospero: 'Tis new to thee.

'Tis new to thee.

"This is the last of the great confrontations of The Tempest. *Miranda is facing a gang of villains. One of them twelve years ago deprived her father of his throne. Another broke his word as an ally. Yet another had raised his sword against his brother, only a little while ago. Prospero has only a very brief reply to make. But how much bitter wisdom is there in this reply. Four words is all that Shakespeare needs here."*

Jan Kott, *Shakespeare Our Contemporary*, 1965

Alonso is unsure whether Miranda is human or divine:

Alonso: ... Is she the goddess that hath severed us
And brought us thus together?
Ferdinand: Sir, she is mortal,
But by immortal providence she's mine;
I chose her when I could not ask my father
For his advice, nor thought I had one. She
Is daughter to this famous Duke of Milan ...

Alonso wishes to ask Miranda for her forgiveness; as an infant, she was cast out of Milan along with her father. But it is time to forgive and forget, insists Prospero, and they must put past wrongs behind them.

Gonzalo, almost overcome with emotion, believes that divine intervention must have played a part in events. They have come from the wedding of the King's daughter, and now, on the same journey, his son too will be married. All around, harmony is being restored:

Gonzalo: Look down, you gods,
And on this couple drop a blessed crown,
For it is you that have chalked forth the way [1]
Which brought us hither ...
... set it down
With gold on lasting pillars: in one voyage
Did Claribel her husband find at Tunis;
And Ferdinand, her brother, found a wife
Where he himself was lost; Prospero his dukedom [2]
In a poor isle; and all of us ourselves,
When no man was his own.

[1] *marked out the path*
[2] *found his dukedom*

The King takes the young couple's hands, and wishes them joy.

News from the King's ship

Ariel returns, invisible to all but Prospero. He is followed by the master and the boatswain of the King's ship, who are in a state of confusion, unsure what power is guiding them.

Gonzalo is delighted to see them. He remembers how, at the height of the terrible storm, he remarked, jokingly, that the boatswain's destiny was to hang for his lack of respect, not to drown. The man is not disrespectful or blaspheming now, on dry land, observes Gonzalo; in fact, he is so perplexed that he can hardly speak. Eventually the boatswain reveals that, in addition to the miraculous escape of the ship's passengers, the ship itself is in perfect condition:

Gonzalo:	I prophesied, if a gallows were on land
	This fellow could not drown …
	… not an oath on shore?
	Hast thou no mouth by land? What is the news?
Boatswain:	The best news is that we have safely found
	Our King and company. The next: our ship,
	Which but three glasses since we gave out split,[1]
	Is tight and yare[2] and bravely rigged as when
	We first put out to sea.

[1] *just three hours ago we believed to have broken apart*
[2] *watertight and seaworthy*

... but three glasses since ...

"Few plays are so haunted by the passing of time as The Tempest: *it has derived even its name from a word (the Latin* tempestas*) which means time as well as tempest."*

Northrop Frye, Introduction to the Pelican edition of *The Tempest*, 1969

The boatswain is not sure how he and the master came to join the royal party. He remembers that the crew were all sleeping soundly below decks when they were woken by a bizarre assortment of unearthly noises. On rising, they scarcely had time to appreciate their wondrously restored ship when somehow, in a dreamlike state, they were transported to join the present company.

Ariel proudly reminds his master that this was all his work. Prospero assures his spirit that his service is greatly appreciated.

Alonso is convinced that some supernatural power is at work in all these events, and is keen to investigate further. Prospero, however, advises against it. Everything will become clear in due course, but for now he should remain carefree and simply enjoy the present: besides, Prospero points out, the royal party is not yet complete.

Looking to the future

Prospero has yet another errand for Ariel. This time, he sends his servant to fetch Caliban, Stephano and Trinculo. Following their failed bid to assassinate Prospero and take over the island, Prospero had them hunted by spirits in the shape of hounds, and tormented with cramps and bruises. The three of them can now be released from their suffering, he tells Ariel.

A moment later, Stephano and Trinculo stagger in, still drunk, wearing the gaudy clothes which Prospero had hung out to distract them from their mission. Stephano is panicking wildly at the sight of the assembled company, while Trinculo, equally befuddled, is pleased to see his fellow passengers.

Caliban, for his part, is impressed by this unprecedented gathering of people. However, the sight of his master Prospero, now wearing his fine robes as the restored Duke of Milan, is daunting; punishment for his disloyalty is surely inevitable.

The King eventually recognises his butler Stephano and his jester Trinculo. He wonders how, even on this remote island, they have managed to get blind drunk:

Alonso: Where should they
              Find this grand liquor that hath gilded 'em? [1]
              How cam'st thou in this pickle? [2]
Trinculo: I have been in such a pickle since I saw you last,
              that I fear me will never out of my bones. I shall
              not fear fly-blowing. [3]

[1] *caused their faces to flush*
[2] *predicament; soaking in alcohol*
[3] *my body is so drenched in liquor that, when
     I die, it will not be infested with flies*

Prospero now turns to Caliban: however, the expected reprimand does not come. Instead, to Caliban's relief, his master asks him and his new companions to prepare Prospero's lodgings for the new visitors. Caliban bitterly regrets his involvement with Stephano and Trinculo:

Prospero: Go, sirrah, to my cell;
              Take with you your companions. As you look
              To have my pardon, trim[1] it handsomely.
Caliban: Ay, that I will; and I'll be wise hereafter
              And seek for grace.[2] What a thrice-double ass
              Was I to take this drunkard for a god,
              And worship this dull fool!

[1] *arrange, decorate*
[2] *mercy, favour*

Prospero invites his guests to stay on the island tonight. This evening, he promises, they will hear all about his adventures since he was expelled from Milan all those years ago.

Tomorrow the royal ship will resume its voyage. Alonso will return to his kingdom; and Prospero, after his daughter's wedding, will at last go back to Milan, where he intends to spend the rest of his days:

> Prospero: ... in the morn
> I'll bring you to your ship, and so to Naples,
> Where I have hope to see the nuptial
> Of these our dear-beloved solemnized;
> And thence retire me to my Milan, where
> Every third thought shall be my grave.

The Tempest was Shakespeare's last major play. In the following years, he worked intermittently with a younger playwright, John Fletcher, but he would never again reach the heights of his earlier creativity. His working life had been spent mainly in London, but by now, approaching the age of fifty, he was increasingly spending his time at his family home in Stratford-upon-Avon.

It is tempting to see parallels between Prospero's return to Milan and the author's own return to the town of his birth:

"It has long been part of the myth of Shakespeare's biography that he made his farewell in The Tempest: *it represents the journey home, the comforting idea that after all the storms he returns to his garden and has a last few happy years in retirement, the great soul at peace. Yet we have no evidence for his state of mind at this moment, and strictly speaking* The Tempest *was not his last play, for three collaborations followed. Nonetheless, it was his last work as sole author; and it seems to have been written at the time when evidence from a London court case establishes his address as Stratford-upon-Avon. And for a writer as intelligent, and as conscious of the illusion of theatre, as he was, it is hardly possible that an autobiographical edge to the plot was not in his mind."*

Michael Wood, *In Search of Shakespeare*, 2003

The rest of their voyage will be untroubled, promises Prospero. In fact they will make such good progress that they will catch up with the remainder of the fleet, which – believing the King's ship to have been destroyed in the tempest – is now on its way home to Naples.

Prospero turns to the invisible Ariel. Giving them fair weather and favourable winds for their journey, he tells the spirit, will be his final task. Then he will at last be free:

> *Alonso:*   I long
>   To hear the story of your life, which must
>   Take the ear strangely.[1]
> *Prospero:*   I'll deliver all,[2]
>   And promise you calm seas, auspicious gales,
>   And sail so expeditious[3] that shall catch
>   Your royal fleet far off. [*aside to Ariel*] My Ariel, chick,
>   That is thy charge. Then to the elements
>   Be free, and fare thou well!
>
> [1] *captivate the listener wonderfully*
> [2] *tell you everything*
> [3] *such a swift voyage*

For the last time, Ariel leaves to do his master's bidding. Prospero then turns back to his companions, and invites them into his lodgings: he has many stories to tell.

"Even Prospero, the agent of transformation in others, is not immune to change ... he has undergone a series of changes: from a student of magic, he became a seeker of revenge through it, and finally he has found his way to a transcendence of it. At the end he abandons his godlike status on the island and, embracing his own humanity, returns to Milan ... Like the others, he is subject to alteration in the depths of his being. These processes of transfiguration enact human possibilities; while The Tempest *points out the clay of which we are made, it also insists on our divine potential."*

Charles Boyce, *Shakespeare A to Z*, 1990

Prospero asks for our help

Alone on the stage, Prospero appeals to the audience. His magical powers are all gone, and the illusions are over. It is no longer Prospero but the spectators who are in command; we have the power – with our cheering and applause – to bring the story to an end, set Prospero free from his island, and release the actor from his role.

Prospero's project of regaining his Dukedom has succeeded; but whether the actor's project of pleasing the audience has also succeeded is something that the spectators, not the magician, must decide.

Prospero: Now my charms are all o'erthrown,
And what strength I have's mine own,
Which is most faint. Now, 'tis true
I must be here confined by you,
Or sent to Naples. Let me not,
Since I have my dukedom got
And pardoned the deceiver, dwell
In this bare island by your spell;
But release me from my bands [1]
With the help of your good hands.
Gentle breath of yours my sails
Must fill, or else my project fails,
Which was to please. Now I want [2]
Spirits to enforce, art to enchant …

[1] *bonds, constraints*
[2] *lack*

Prospero asks us to be lenient in our judgement if anything in the play has displeased us. We all, in the end, desire forgiveness for our faults:

Prospero: As you from crimes would pardoned be,
Let your indulgence set me free.

––––––––
––––––

Acknowledgements

The following publications have proved invaluable as sources of factual information and critical insight:

- Jonathan Bate, *Soul of the Age*, Penguin Books, 2009

- Charles Boyce, *Shakespeare A to Z*, Roundtable Press, 1990

- Nicholas Fogg, *Hidden Shakespeare*, Amberley Publishing, 2013

- Northrop Frye, *On Shakespeare*, Yale University Press, 1986

- Northrop Frye, Introduction to the Pelican edition of *The Tempest*, 1969

- Harold C. Goddard, *The Meaning of Shakespeare*, University of Chicago Press, 1951

- Andrew Gurr, *Playgoing in Shakespeare's London*, Cambridge University Press, 1996

- G. B. Harrison, *Introducing Shakespeare*, Penguin Books, 1966

- Jan Kott, *Shakespeare Our Contemporary*, Doubleday, 1965

- Laurie Maguire and Emma Smith, *30 Great Myths About Shakespeare*, Wiley-Blackwell, 2013

- James Shapiro, *1606: William Shakespeare and the Year of Lear*, Faber & Faber, 2015

- Lytton Strachey, *Shakespeare's Final Period*, published in *The Independent Review*, 1904

- Virginia Mason Vaughan and Alden T. Vaughan, Introduction to the Arden edition of *The Tempest*, 1999

- *The Cambridge History of English and American Literature*, edited by A.W. Ward and A. R. Waller, Cambridge University Press, 1921

- Michael Wood, *In Search of Shakespeare*, BBC Books, 2003

All quotations from *The Tempest* are taken from the Arden Shakespeare.

Guides currently available in the *Shakespeare Handbooks* series are:

- ❑ **Antony & Cleopatra** (ISBN 978 1 899747 02 3, £4.95)

- ❑ **As You Like It** (ISBN 978 1 899747 00 9, £4.95)

- ❑ **Hamlet** (ISBN 978 1 899747 07 8, £4.95)

- ❑ **Henry IV, Part 1** (ISBN 978 1 899747 05 4, £4.95)

- ❑ **King Lear** (ISBN 978 1 899747 03 0, £4.95)

- ❑ **Macbeth** (ISBN 978 1 899747 04 7, £4.95)

- ❑ **A Midsummer Night's Dream** (ISBN 978 1 899747 09 2, £4.95)

- ❑ **Romeo & Juliet** (ISBN 978 1 899747 10 8, £4.95)

- ❑ **The Tempest** (ISBN 978 1 899747 08 5, £4.95)

- ❑ **Twelfth Night** (ISBN 978 1 899747 01 6, £4.95)

www.shakespeare-handbooks.com

Prices correct at time of going to press. Whilst every effort is made to keep prices low, Upstart Crow Publications reserves the right to show new retail prices on covers which may differ from those previously advertised in the text or elsewhere.